In Fields of Dandelions

Previous iUniverse Publications—poetry

I Swim Seas of Thirty-Two Legions, November 2002
The Talisman Pick—"Voices and Hats," December 2002
The Land of the Frogs—"Seas of Green," February 2003

Hilltop Records, CA—
Lyrics/poems from I Swim Seas of Thirty-Two Legions
Featured on CD release "America," April 2003

Titles—*Time Stood Still for the Moment & Like a Child's Book*

Dorrance Publishing—pre-k children's book
Around the World with Rosalie, May 2003

In Fields of Dandelions

Plucked is the Poet's Paintbrush

Christine Redman-Waldeyer

iUniverse, Inc.
New York Lincoln Shanghai

In Fields of Dandelions
Plucked is the Poet's Paintbrush

iUniverse books may be ordered through booksellers or by contacting:

iUniverse
2021 Pine Lake Road, Suite 100
Lincoln, NE 68512
www.iuniverse.com
1-800-Authors (1-800-288-4677)

ISBN-13: 978-0-595-28267-8
ISBN-10: 0-595-28267-9

Printed in the United States of America

For my teachers
All the world's people and creatures
And for Joey and Jessica
Who give me sight through children's eyes

Contents

Contents

Foreword

If you read only one book of poetry this year, or haven't read one in years, *In Fields of Dandelions* should be the one. This short volume is a gem that speaks to the beauty and wonder of everyday experiences. The poems are witty, thought-provoking, inspiring, and touching. They deal with teaching and learning, love lost and found, lust, parenting, childhood, gifts and reversals, race, opportunities, and the destruction of war. The poems touch on timely topics but also look at the universal issues that shape our lives. I found the book hard to put down. The poems are never dry or stuffy; instead they touch at our lives and hearts. Each one leaves the reader yearning for more. The author, Christine Waldeyer-Redman, is an insightful teacher, and indeed a philosopher, whose poems teach so much more than any lecture could. This is not a book of simple platitudes, but a collection of thought-provoking pieces that will make the reader reexamine his or her own life and experiences, laugh at shared joys, and remember old disappointments. The author's writing is clever, insightful, and inspiring. The poems are an excellent selection of Christine Waldeyer-Redman's latest work. In a poem titled "The Awakening", she writes "It was by the grace of God I fell into teaching." We should be thankful that Christine has graced us with this fine book of her work. It is a gem. I recommend it heartily.

By Richard Veit, Ph.D.
Department of History and Anthropology, Monmouth University
Author of *Digging New Jersey's Past: Historical Archaeology in the Garden State*

Foreword

The relationship between the natural world and those occupying it forms the basis for this intriguing collection of lyrical poems by Christine Redman-Waldeyer. In this world, which is growing increasingly smaller, foreign influences exert major and far-reaching impact upon indigenous cultures and environments. Some may argue that this is the inevitable toll of progress, an element of human history from time immemorial. Our ever-increasing knowledge of the natural world has revealed the life-sustaining importance of once-pristine places such as rain forests and coastal marshes. As satellites orbit this blue miracle, planet Earth, no geographic point is immune from being mapped, described, or targeted in some way. I am reminded of an observation made some years ago by Margaret Meade at my Barnard College graduation, that our ancient ancestors had no way of knowing that they were facing extinction. Armed with our growing scientific knowledge of human impact on the environment, what priorities have we established, and what legacy will we leave future generations who will inhabit this planet we share?

The poems in this collection delight in the revelation of the wonders of the natural world. Inspired by travels to Jamaica, the author, guided by life-long residents, explored still-wild regions and was inspired by their beauty, untamed, complex and mysterious. These places are revered by people who do not own them, but who respect them and have come to derive natural and spiritual benefits from them. The author sought out these still-pristine, exotic places, which have somehow escaped the eviscerating effect resort development has wrought on portions of the native environment.

Through her unique perspective, the author presents a view of external and inner states, using the delicate balance of nature and our effect on it as a departure point for her writing. Her role as an educator and mother also inform her writing. The role of intuition and the vital connection between the environment and our physical and emotional well-being is underscored in her viewpoint.

Readers will be transported, inspired and challenged by the journey related in these pages.

By Patricia Florio Colrick

Biographical notes on Patricia Florio Colrick

Patricia Florio Colrick, a design historian and preservationist, resides in Spring Lake with her husband and three children. She is the owner of the Landmark Bookstores in Spring Lake. She is the author of books on Spring Lake, Hoboken and Montville in the Arcadia Publishing Images of America series, served as editor of two centennial books for St. Catharine's Church in Spring Lake. She is also a contributor to several architectural entries in the forthcoming Encyclopedia of New Jersey.

Preface

The first time I questioned beauty, really questioned the meaning of it was when my three-year old daughter brought me a bouquet of dandelions hand picked and choice. Her older brother led the way to which flowers held the right length stems, to which were the brightest yellows. And displayed brilliantly in a glass was this bouquet on my kitchen table. She had yet to learn that these treasures were considered weeds.

Neighbors kindly coaxed my children to wander and pick the weeds from their lawns, which became a silent joke acknowledged by a smile between adults. I silently joked to myself and wondered if the flowers could be encouraged to grow. What if I became the first radical homeowner to purposely harvest fields of dandelions? In a way, I do still contribute to their seeding. Even as an adult who can help to pick one of the stems holding the white and wispy cotton balls and blow wishes. I remember my best friend now nearly thirty years ago teaching me the magic of wishes upon this white puff carrying seeds. He was also the friend who taught me if you held a buttercup under one's chin that you could tell if one liked butter by whether or not their skin captured the glow of the flower. I'm not sure where he picked up the great knowledge of these children's rituals. The rituals seemingly passed from one generation to another. It is a great right of a child to believe in the magic of nature. It is a right of the imagination, I would happily pass the knowledge on for my own children.

I considered the beauty of the dandelion, which is the highly sought foe of the many who take pride in their lawns. I admire its strength against adults whom they happily provided wishes for, whom now return the gift with pesticides. The dandelion smiles on. For there will always be children and adults such as myself who never grow up. I love our loathed weed. For it as yellow as the sun and in death is as white as the clouds against blue skies. I admire its fight to survive. For in one puff, in one death, the many seeds into the winds are blown.

It was not shortly thereafter, that I had been presented with the first wild bouquet of spring that I left for a trip to Jamaica. It was in this island, which holds much history and ghosts of horrific pasts, that I encountered a people much like these dandelions. An island that lost its native Indian population to smallpox by European encounters, an island in which thousands of African slaves were put to work on the sugarcane plantations in 18th century. The same island would continue in abuses well after emancipation in early 19th century, using imported Indians and Chinese as indentured servants after losing the many African workers.

It was an island once wild in beauty but groomed to meet the needs or wants or expectations of others. Like the dandelions, this island was weeded, groomed to fit a time period in which European countries competed in trade. Much like our lawns weeded and groomed to fit the expectations of our little communities who compete on smaller scales. It is the availability of pesticides at every turn that propagates this competition.

I learned much of the history not from books but from the men and women of the island who happily answered my many questions. I also learned that beaches were not all that natural. That the wild vines, palms, and wild herbs used by their grandparents' generation in teas for healing and strength properties were cut back for resorts. Many spoke of the continuous building of resorts by outsiders, a fear that the island would succumb and be overridden was clear. At first I shrank in disgust, but realized I was also part of the problem. I had paid to stay at one of these resorts. I admit to being one who utilizes these resorts as a means to get places but winds up spending much time away from the resort itself. It is not just my need to feel the real culture and people, but also a need to step away from the much-abused buffet tables laid out. Never was I one to relax after I found myself guilty of overfilling my plate, only to leave much behind.

While the resorts provide work for an island of people considered poverty stricken, I can't help to think back to its origins. While I had not found successive generations of the very first natives, I had found men as wild and strong growing much like the dandelions in the mountains of Jamaica. It was in the waterfalls I was led by a man named Dennis. His hair held some gray in its black, but his body was as strong as any twenty year olds. We were to walk the rock filled downhill river about a mile. I hesitated watching the rolling waterfalls and questioned this trek with a three and five-year old. It had not taken long for me to relax as I watched Dennis lead us with my highly advanced and expensive camera in one hand and a more expensive commodity, my daughter in the other, barefoot and like a fish to water. This in comparison to our water shoes and our clumsy stumble through the rocks. The river to Dennis and many of the other teachers of the land I met had made the waterfalls their art. I highly respected their art and thought to my personal art of words.

As Dennis followed the trail of water, he also brought to our attention the river's water life of crawfish, snails, and the sucker fish we see in pet shops. On the trail back to the grounds, he pointed out the mango, banana, and bit through a plant which opened up to cocoa seeds, which delighted my son who learned this is where chocolate stems from. We learned the spice curry came from a plant that looked very much like carrot.

It occurred to me that Dennis was a teacher of his art, with a born knowledge of the water and land. It is here, I made a conscious decision to learn the names of those who taught me along the way. Being a teacher myself, I was blinded to the fact that teachers are not only those who hold esteemed degrees and spoke to classrooms. These names were as esteemed. On the many travels in past to the islands of Greece, Puerto Rico, St. Bartholomew's, St. Martin's, Aruba, and off Mexico lost were the names of my many teachers.

I learned about the peanie wallies, a lightening bug of the island whose tail did not light but their feelers or eyes did instead. This I learned from a security guard named O'Neil Whyte on the beaches of Negril who claimed you could see these bugs coming from miles away. He spoke of the crickets' song and the sting of white ants. When he learned I was writing of his island, he asked that I include his name and wrote I did on a scrap of paper found floating in my purse. He was sure to spell his last name, which required a "y" instead of the common "i." I learned that yes, indeed, these teachers, too want to be known.

I learned from a tourist driver named Orville, also on the beaches of Negril, the many wild plants his grandmother used for teas. Well-built, he proudly announced that he did not use any artificial chemicals but gained strength from his grandmother's old recipes. He taught me the name of the black dove crowned white who sat outside my veranda every morning, deemed the bald-plated dove for his soft white crown. He taught me that the original shores carried much of the wild plant now set back, shored off for our sunbathing leisure.

I learned from our tour bus driver, Roman, a Jamaican of Indian descent how his ancestors came to be part of this island. I learned from him also the philosophy of the Rastafarians. True Rastafarians were those dedicated to everything natural. From a man named Kevin, I learned of the seven-mile long cave where bones of Indians diseased with small pox were found. The same cave held a history in which the Spanish fled from attacks of the English in the 17th century, to a later date, when slaves hid from their English masters in hope to find their way to the mountains for freedom.

I admit to not acquiring all names, as I learned or unlearned from an awkward confrontation of teachers who presented themselves as a couple I presumed French by their language. Back at the resort, my son had taken to playing with what was presumably meant for washing feet. Fascinated by the descend of the water to the ocean, he would turn the fountain of water on and run along with its flow until it reached the ocean. I stood by and watched casually, as I felt he was learning from the experience. He noted the branches of river that broke off to which he named the triangles and asked if the Mountain Rivers also reached the ocean. At one of these playtimes, the male presence of the couple with determination and intent got up and turned the water off in front of me. Shortly after, the female scolded my son upon his return to let the gates of water flow again. In broken English she said, "Only for washing feet!" I understood completely.

I wasn't sure if I should feel ashamed or angry. On one hand, yes, it was a waste of water as I come from a land of plenty and easily forgot my world community. On the other hand, I could not help to hope upon hope that perhaps this is the making of a to be scientist at play. This was the same child who combed the beaches for land crabs and the woods for the yellow boa, once a thriving species of Jamaica. Is not children's play the practice and perfection of the making of adults? It was a hard coin to flip? Perhaps between my unidentified teachers and myself there may have been an exchange of visions?

A similar experience happened in the mountains as we openly slathered our bodies with sun block and were stopped immediately by one of the trail guides. "No need, there is shade in the mountains and this hurts the fishes eyes!" While stopping immediately and wiping the remnants of the poison from our skins, I had been brought to a much larger scale.

A scale that made me take a hard long look at what we as a global community have done to our ozone layer, polluting it to a point that it is dangerously cancerous to bare it the sun's rays alone. Yet instead of escaping the sun, we put ourselves directly in it, hoping to acquire the vacationers' much beloved tan while adding more poison to nature. The poison did not stop at the eyes of the mountain fish but also are poisoning our sea faring friends.

Have we nearly plucked but all our dandelions' friends? It was the ride to the airport that answered this question emphatically. Throughout the vacation, I was taken from learning experience to learning experience in an air-conditioned van with tinted windows to keep shade. The last ride, however, to the airport lacked that experience entirely.

Upon entering our pickup van, you knew immediately this was not going to be the ride of comfort. Out of the testimony of complete truth, which only a child can give, did my son comment on the condition of the vehicle. We were then met by an angry old man who drove us an hour and half back with the windows open, flying through Jamaica's rough highways at enormous speeds. Oddly, I was thankful for the ride, probably not as thankful as I would have been had I not had my three and five-year old at my side, especially with a lack of seatbelts. Nevertheless, the driver without hesitation picked up Jamaican workers who needed rides home away from the resorts and into the cities. Here I saw not only the land now brighter through open windows, but also how the people of the resorts who served us actually lived. Regret now sank, as I remembered back to the partaking of my children with other vacationers' children, to the endless emptying of the fruit bar's slush machines. Had we gone mad in the inherited belief of a vacationer's rights and had this been passed to our children?

I met another teacher, a young woman in her early twenties who waitressed at one of the hotels, named Shekita. Conversation started with her love of my daughter's long blond curls and blue eyes. I commented on the beauty of the island and told her I was a teacher and had a few Jamaican born students back in the states. I shook my head in wonderment announcing out loud a lack of understanding why anyone would want to leave. She answered immediately; it was the lack of opportunities. It occurred to me that the trade was the beauty of the island for education and careers. I wondered if I could exchange my comfort of opportunities for the simple beauty of this island. We both came to no answers. Do we only seek what we feel deprived of?

I found this question reflects my poetry. The poetry comments on the deprivation of the soul, our spiritual awareness, our surroundings, our social condition, our environment, and in our quest for love and forgiveness. As people, we are like the dandelions. Fearing death we bequest and blow our many seeds. Strong-willed, we root where we please. We can also smile bright as the yellow sun in empowerment. In my child's hands were the many dandelions held in smaller worlds. In my hands, the wild dandelions picked, are the inspiration for this bouquet of poetry.

While reading this bouquet I have gathered from my surroundings and from life experience itself, one may find a certain theme throughout this work consisting of references to blue or white lights. These lights are felt if seen in an ethereal way is a self-recognition of love or the higher self. More than auras spoken of, they are shown to us with true sense of our higher selves or the trueness of love.

In other words, it is a sign of awakening. Dreams and lights are a consciousness very real to me and often this is reflected in my poetry.

A special thank you to a close friend who called me one winter morning to wake me to a world glowing in the aftermath of an ice storm. The trees were eerily beautiful, covered as if in glass with morning light dancing off the clarity. It was this wake up call that allowed for me to see that with every storm comes beauty. While pointing out the obvious to me, this friend was my motivator to write. That morning is reflected in my poem, *Glass Trees (From Reaches of Winter's Nip)*. Allow me to be your motivator as I had been blessed with a wonderful friend as mine, the motivator to open your eyes to the obvious beauty that surrounds us all.

1

*To be a Child Left with Nothing but
the Grasp of Butterflied Dreams*

As Tape Sewed the Seams

In bliss he sat with silver sheers
in hand.
And to linoleum floors
Hamilton in green did land.

And my red turned to green
as taped sewed the seams.

To be a child left with nothing
but the grasp of butterflied dreams.

Dandelion Bouquet

Running through untrimmed grass
she picked at the dandelions,
carrying a fistful of yellow fun.

She had yet to learn
that her bouquet
was already deemed ugly.

And I wondered to the field
that lay before me.
Who determined they were none?

And quiet I kept
for I would not deliver
what was undone.

The Princess

The soft reds played on yellows weaved into braids.
I looked down upon this little head
whose freckles danced on white skin.

She asked if she could be
a princess like me.
A princess?

I looked woefully at my own clothes
to which no princess would wear.
A princess? Like me?
She nodded and took my hand.

Pulled was I to a picture
that now blended to the wall to me.
Yet shined in white with gown to her.

I smiled and ran my hand
through those strawberry highlights.
Yes, you can be like me.
She danced in glee and through closets
we rustled to pull a dress to sparkle as she.

Through her which had been long forgotten
sparkled I did in my memories.
To think I played a princess
on a snowy bell toned day.

She taught me it did not have to end.
I too still can play.
For didn't I that day?

Her Garden

She spoke of the rocks
collected from all her travels.
All which are laid in her garden.
A reminder of what she has seen.

And time withers away
but never is forgotten,
the destination of those that shine.

He listened to the story told by his teacher.
And from his travels walked the walls of his backyard.
He brought his rocks for her to keep.

Rocks without the glimmer
but in the ordinary to her, to him did shine.

Fountain Play

Grew short the day
and the taste of salt
stung the skin's say
with waves no longer sought.

Last of the day
when reds slipped behind seas.
And rest turned to more play
with feet under free.

And dance did virgin feet
under the cool waters
of fountain's meet,
with a catching of heavy droplet's lure.

With fountain play
enraptured
was he by river's break away,
through which small lands punctured.

Coursing triangles
toward salted banks
entangled
briefly in beach's ranks.

And he followed his river
with breath and flesh in shivers
till fresh water met salt.
And bigger worlds were caught.

—Children at play at the feet washer
Negril Beach, Jamaica

The Dandelions' Dance

Picked I did two dandelions
for her to give.

And to the car radio the little suns beat.

Danced they did in her two little hands,
until the green stems limped.

2

The Men of the Falls

Instruments of a One-Man Band

A poet is a one-man band
playing the instrument of surroundings.

To the Sound of the Yellow Grass Melody

The air was crisp and the click of boots hit cement.
The rubbing of leather sounded off cold airs.

But silenced was my walk
to the sound of those with webbed feet.
Those nipping at earth's yellowed grasses.
The sound in a Rhythm set to a peaceful melody.

I stopped to watch close the orchestra of nature's musicians,
as an unseen audience.
Unseen except by one, which looked me in the eye.

Strong was his black face and although beautiful
instinct served it to protect.
But in permission, I was only given a quick stare.
For a few more seconds of this eternity,
I took in the strip of the yellowed grasses' melody.

The click of boots hit cement
as the rubbing of leathers sounded off cold airs.

Glass Trees (From Reaches of Winter's Nip)

One short night
and I awaken and see.
Awaken to dazzling light
dancing off glass trees.

Like a wonderland,
against snowy plains
these glass trees stand.
Casting, I box and frame
this canvas…

Light dances off nature's glass
of Ice
as branches dance in wind's pass
Slice.

And I box the dance of iced melody
Crackling
in what was heaven's sea
Tickling.
From reaches of winter's nip
airs still chill but deep I sip.

—*March 2003'*
   After an ice-storm

In Emma's Hands

In Emma's hands
the starfish green
spread its fan,
and many feet did stream.

In Emma's hands
Jamaica's starfish green
did glide on white-skinned land,
making blue eyes beam.

And carefully those eyes
did scan
vast ocean mirroring blue sky,
holding what shines wet with salted sand.

And deep we swam
to hideaway
in Great plan,
the creature's return to play.

In Emma's hands
drifted did the star to salt-touched land.
Masked it was in currents' blizzard seas,
released from Emma's hands free.

And on this starfish
grant we did upon the many of God's wish.

—Jamaica—5/20/03
  For the Green Starfish

Purple Star

I walked the floor,
with toes touching sands of coral reef.

And alone amongst this vast white floor,
eyes did catch a purple star.

Seen through waters clear and blue.
Seen through waters dusted with sands askew.

And wait I did for clear tides,
to reach and grasp what shined.

I did lay it in my hands and watch its many feet,
clinging to this foreign land.

Oh Purple Star! You shine more alive.
And returned I did you, to this sea of sky.

And alone amongst this vast white floor,
eyes did catch a purple star.

—Jamaica—2003
  For the Purple Starfish

To Reason

Surrounded by resorts,
I walked along their beaches.
I met a man named Orville,
black as night, with graying hair.

He spoke of a place
where people still reasoned.
Here we might call it debate.

He spoke of a time when his Chinese,
high-school teacher spent hours outside classes.
Hours spent with students sitting and reasoning.

But as his story grew, all those who governed
reasoned.
Reasoned his reasoning classes should stop!

—*Jamaica—2003*

Master Artist

Surrounded by resorts seemingly beautiful,
taking in the nature, I walked along their beaches.
I met a man named Orville,
black as night, with graying hair.

He spoke of a time when the bush
came to the water's edge, then of a time
it was cut away.

I then realized I am taking part
in the destruction, the destruction of our Master Artist.
An artist still who has no contemporaries and no rivals.
An artist that none can emulate

—*Jamaica, May 2003*

Wilton's Walking Sticks

In airs cooled
we raced through
on wheels tooled,
not knowing the winds that blew.

For rest we withdrew
from sped away
rides of swaying palms' views,
and from Billie goats' play.

And approached we were
by a whittling man
holding music in scraping whir,
against bamboo's stretch of land.

And hands worked
begged more than words
to look
at the craft of the poor man's world.

It was not pity
that emptied pockets of US green
but the escape from what is city,
the cries of many means.

I asked the name
of the Whittling man
and Wilton fit just sane,
and fingers to grasp green fanned.

And for my children
two walking sticks

carved with faces of holy men,
in small fingers stood thick.

And carved I knew I would
his name
that Whittling Wilton stood,
for he spoke for the poor man's plane.

—*5/19/03—Jamaica*
At Christopher Columbus' Landing

The Men of the Falls

The mountains
so green
billowed nature's fountains.
The mountains so serene…

And men dark and barefoot
did gleam,
under bamboo shoots
from the river that streams.

And through the falls
they carried
even the small,
married.

Married to the land,
for the land spanned
as third and fourth hands,
working through uncarved paths planned.

The Men of the Falls'
cuts sank not in feet,
but in their builds lean and tall
carved by nature's seat.

The Men of the Falls
were fish to water,
were the songs to birds' calls.
To what is earthly matter…

But unlike these men to the falls
stood the name of our leader's call
menacing,
for his name was Dennis.

—*5/19/03—Jamaica*

3

The Witch's Flight Broke
Falling into his Dreams

The Good Witch

And over his storm, the witch's flight broke,
falling into his dreams.

On Ropes of Hair

I had wondered to my need
to grow the locks long.
Like an unkept weed
that doesn't belong.

And in this tower
no want of shears,
I sought something of power,
something to swipe the tears.

And after years of kept,
a knight crossed the window below.
And curious up the long rope he crept
and held me till my heart was sewn.

And a knowing he could not stay
in balls too clear,
I could see myself pray
to the winds I feared.

And I begged of him
to grow
his locks to winds' swim.
For hard these winds would blow…

And left he did,
and the storms grew wild.
And out my window, fingers bid
his hair of the Nile.

And holding on to strands too few,
I'm weathering the storms' darkest blues.

A Mile Walked in Bare Feet

The path is long and hard
and I've walked already a thousand steps.
The earth is what is bard
and to heart is kept.

And so long this walk,
crumbled had my leaning stick.
But along the way winds softly talk.
And stepped I did upon a musician's pick.

The music so beautiful, the colors so bright,
almost it did not seem real.
I had kicked at this odd sight,
but stepping over I could feel.

I looked behind
and returned to its fight.
To my heart it pined,
for life had taken on in this extinguished light.

For the path
it had lain to be run by wheels
with earth to scathe.
I would steal...

And in this pick hung,
faceless it certainly had not become.
For a knight appeared to strum,
and hands glided over a wooden sun.

And to his music,
and to her song,
bare feet to earth did not burn long.

A mile walked in bare feet
became a journey were the two shall meet.
And to his music and to her song
became a journey forever sweet.

She walked a mile in bare feet,
and it became *their* journey were the two shall meet.

—4/24/03

Dream House

The drive, the dream
relived one crisp winter night
shimmered, gleamed
on a lake, in my heart under this light.

The moon full heightened,
flooding a young woman's once fantasy.
Mood lightened…
and near him, age swept away.

Stopping in front of a cast of rooms
holding to many histories,
my dreams once again bloomed.
On bedroom doors swung, overlook one would,
    to a domed ministry.

I pictured spring
over the frozen lake.
The greens, the murmur of Wings,
rushing in to take.

Both in home and nature,
a dream that holds what is rich.
Sinking, lifting what holds to stature,
seeking across church bells' pitch.

I took this drive young and foolishly
with another young female friend
drinking in a surreal ecstasy,
to which nothing would we tend.

I drive still dreaming,
but passing over old dreams.

I watched him cast his eyes
over my dream's untold ties.

Changed I did my dreams' key,
for rich I'd be
to catch his cast and release
what is laden free.

Running from room to room
seeking out *his* mysteries.
The only cost to find this ministry,
I found this night under the glow of the moon.

In Dreams...towards each other we Run

In dreams towards each other we run.
By day we live in these shadows,
holding to these dreams and sing of their notions.

But I wonder between us,
How many lies exist?

And we lie both knowing truth would carry pain.
The only truth is love and in this, for this, we lie.

Siempre Angelo, Siempre
(Always Angel, Always)

My words sit in what storms
but by my will.

Should they be torn
by the rains, the sleet never still;
still what may blur
Keeps.
They drown in what stirs
Deep.

Hold to your heart
words clear.
Only death could part,
carry no fear.

Lifetimes past
and now with you I found my peace,
my rest.
Know this will last,
siempre angelo, siempre.

The Eventual Descend

A reach from my fingertips,
but not to escape completely.
Towards the larger skies you do not fly.
Still you reach ceilings all too high,
and the string dangles so.

And I pray my patience wins
for its eventual descend.
For I close my eyes and the balloon
becomes him.

Like a child I cry,
and beneath use little feet
to jump, to bait,
in my impatience to wait.

Still I Soar

Today the sun hit my skin
and I took in the flowers' bloom,
listening to the music on the radio.

Still I soar!
You have underestimated my strength.
I'll never let you go!

Pretty Feet

In his hands he took my feet,
and declared them unique.
For this pair was pretty.

And considered he did on feet,
this thought rare.

I think it was more than pretty feet.

He held them looking as if they were the bands
that secured diamonds.

For Words of Romance I May be Lost

Perhaps for words of romance I'm lost,
as yesterdays lent to hideaway bliss,
to breathless kiss.

To looks that tingle,
to twilight's twinkle,
to yesterdays' of walks alone,
of quiet talks long gone.

To sweet notes of love,
to hands held tight,
surrounded by your fleshed glove.

Perhaps for words of romance I'm lost.
For no longer are we alone, yet together.
Pitter-patters of little feet sound so new
and just as sweet.

To little eyes and little heads
who sleep in tiny beds.

To what we made,
to what we dreamt,
to all that still we've kept.

To tomorrows' dreams
even through tired eyes that gleam.

To snow that glitters
even off now bent silver.
To a home at times without,
to hands now worked with splinter

Romance may leave but love does not fold to cease.

4

My Senses Wet with Sensual Cue

Something Sung but Yet to Flower

Still hours…
Hours after a touch strong,
something sung but yet to flower
to my flesh longs.

Longs to burst…
Burst to blooms
and I thirst.

I close my eyes and swoon,
for still I feel my breath taken.
Taken from lips sweetly bitter.
Still I gasp from thighs tense shaken,
and thoughts burn to ashes from litter.

For I wade in lust
that calls his name,
forward to my home to thrust.
I redden not in shame
but from zealous blush.

And in my dreams,
I thrust his name
in torrid poetry that screams.
And with my mouth I trace his frame.

The dreams…
the thoughts,
flare blood in streams,
and open, so open to be brought…

And I close my eyes and taste him
and breathless

from breathing sin,
groins do ache for his caress.

Still hours…
Hours after scents, his, hold strong,
something sung but yet to flower,
to my flesh longs.

And the warmth in groins heighten,
and breasts act on winds cool,
as I think, as I sing, as a love-bound fool.

Oh, Island!

You are an island empty of opportunities
but rich in food, in water.

An island I wish to visit more than once.

Sing my Name

Sing my name
and I'd crumble and be yours.
For a heart no longer tame
holds what blurs.

I'd burn it all down
to an ash,
stripped of crowns.
In it I would not thrash
but step out.

Step out to hear you sing my name,
and I would mount new frames.

Chest to Chest, Heart to Heart

They became one.
And after breath once again became light,
they stayed as one talking, neither moving.

They found what was whole,
and to finally rip away seemed wrong.
So they lay chest-to-chest, heart to heart.
So strong the need, once again they became one.

Holding to their own voices,
singing free in the wholeness.

Could it Be?

My breasts ache and I think of the new life
that sits below.
Or is it my imagination?

And I push at a swollen belly
and wait for answers to come in tides that dry.

And I wait…

It is his?
I think of art worked by the love of two artists.

Could it be?
And with breasts sore,
I wait for answers found in tides that dry.

Violet's Blush

Violets
so twisted blue,
caught I am in this perfumed net
of heavenly dew.

And wait I did
for seasons' nuance.
For this flower's bid
of pollinating dance.

Violets
so twisted blue,
my senses wet
with sensual cue.

And twisted blues
in shades of purple gush,
to my blood bedews
of trees so lush.

So twisted, so twisted blue
in this purple blush,
I feel so new…

Buttercup

Buttercup,
I hold you beneath
my chin
in wild belief.

The yellow glows
on lightly weathered skin.
I close my eyes
and feel it spread sin.

Oh, buttercup
yellow and wild,
memories bittersweet
of child.

Oh, buttercup
wild,
on my flesh
you smiled.

Of springs'
dance of dust,
pollinating…
pollinating must.

And dragged
over skin
warm with spring,
held into flesh is your green-stemmed pin.

I Dreamed of Walls

I dreamed of walls but not ones
that lay between us.

I dreamed of ones we rode together in rhythm.
A rocking in communication between souls

5

What Hurts is that Tomorrow's Had Been Long Forgotten

A Young Woman's Tears

Face ruddy,
I can see her tears welting in the corners,
looking for escapes but stand denied.

Not to cry I say and empathize.
I was there too and at times still there.

Be strong for you are young.
Many more will pass by.

Yet even with my eyes dry,
my heart still pangs for loves lost.

Gone today, gone are yesterday's…
But what hurts, is that tomorrows' had been
long forgotten.

Lost in Magic of the Cards

We sat in summer winds
blown in by ocean's tides,
and I read his cards.

He'd fall in love with a friend.
That friend pointed to me,
but these cards spoke.
He would break a heart, his own…

He did fall in love and it was with me.
He broke away senselessly, tragically…

Funny in the magic of the cards,
lost was the fact he would also break me.

The Tides of Fertility

The tides of fertility flowed,
and in this flood I found relief and darkness.
For the same red in my heart
that courses this river's flow,
signifies what could be life.

An art by two artists
who paint with love.
Hold I do to unrequited relief,
and solace is found in the paint
not ready to dry.

Under the Shadow of a Storm Cloud

Like a storm cloud, he carries on,
surfacing under bad winds.

And the winds behind me,
I never can see.

Too fast I turn,
and he strikes with the venom
only storm clouds care.

And jagged is the heat,
that to my flesh, my soul is beat.

And the white light is ugly
to which his mouth can cast.

Like a storm cloud, he carries on,
surfacing under bad winds.

Bald Plated Pedoves

Outside my veranda,
the bald plated pedove cooed.
Strutting black…
cocking his snow topped head.

The strut in his full-fleshed tree
brought in she.
Where she danced in her tree
along the plank of a palm leaf…

—May 2003
Jamaica—Mating Season
for doves nicknamed "Bald Plates"

Dressing for the Dance

Stepping away from the dance floor,
I was approached.
A request to join him for a dinner date

Called beautiful,
still he asked of my unmasked face
and lack of trophied jewels.

Further requests was that I join him
but dressed with the essential tools.

Stepping away from floor of real music,
I was a fool led to another dance of fool's lore.

Dust to My Strings

I am curved, strong in color and beauty,
but stand in lines amongst walls.

The guitarist stirred for the moment,
plucks my strings.
But always searching it is not song,
but dust I see to my strings.

Helpless to move, watching as he
moves amongst the many curved swing.

A Song for Sarah

Sweet life
born in virgin sin.
A chord cut with knife
deep from your momma's bin.

Always lost you drank this passing knight,
and he took you for his wife.
Sweet Sarah's plight...
Did you know into him I breathed life?

Did he tell you?
My heart he stroked.
At his touch my thighs shook throbbing blue.
That I came to him in dreams unbroke.

Did he tell you?
Sweet Sarah,
That I cry for two.
That I always knew.

Sweet Sarah I could be you
or you somber in my shoes.
Oh, Sweet Sarah, I always knew.
Feel the blue Sarah; See the clues.

Sweet Sarah find your day.
Faceless foe, Faceless friend, for you this song I pray.

Is it Cruel Curiosity?

With cruel curiosity you still hold to me,
and I squirm to breathe.

But neither do I let go.
So perhaps in cruel curiosity,
I also hold to you.

Hoping for Crossroads

Searched I did our sanded beaches,
wondering if you too were lonely.

But empty, my walks were unmet.
Though I wonder to paths walked and missed.

Would we ever reach any crossroads?

6

Walls with No Words

Poetaster

I sat with ink to my pen, lost to grief.
For lost was my friend, time too brief.

I sat to write my sorrows away,
and realized the fate which had gone array.

For the shadow of a thief stood as friend.
To my words chief, was a heart full of sin.

Walls with no Words

You've put me in a walled cage
by your silence where lips run dry,
and words cease to run with doors.

And Dance She Could All Day

She pleaded
that I dance with her.
She needed
the dance to purr.

My little one,
I didn't want to say
I dance alone
despite all I pray.

My little one
heard the music play,
heard the sun,
and dance she could all day.

And at my dress she pleaded stay.
Seeded, I became a swing of play

This moment
I swung, swung
her from hands that sent
her to and from.

My little one
heard the music play,
heard the sun,
and dance she could all day.

And cried she did,
Take my hands!
Which from nothing slid
and escaped this land.

And cried she did,
Swing Me, Swing Me!
And with all I could,
in dance for her…I still can see.

I Cry in the Clarity

For the pain my vehicle surmounts,
I react and move mountains.

And with pain of heart,
I seek mending through reason.

They move my heart to move me towards
a calling…

And so clear I see this, I tremble in fear.
For if he was sent as such, my vision steers.

I in anger, in sadness seek their answers.
And whilst no words are spoken out loud,
I do hear.

The vehicle provided by the gods so saddens me,
for I loved him.

And in destinations reached, I wonder in ends.
Should the vehicle's motor stand uncharged and remain
or in constant motion drive away…

Cry I do in the clarity!

The Ceiling Fan

Thought when this did move
by nothing mechanical
that guardians were near.

And every so often with turning panels
would I rejoice!
For death then was nothing to fear.

But…lost I wasn't in the ignorance,
and found it moved when heads were wet,
and with a smaller fan was steered.

Best Friends of Today

They ran the beaches
meeting new friends on holiday.

Friends from across the globes,
friends they called best.

Friends they hadn't realized,
for the moment would only be.

—*Jamaica—May 2003*
  For Joey 5 and his faraway friends

I Pray to Leave Worlds Sane

Suffocated I am under too many degrees.
Suffocated I am in not enough.
My voice seeks air for lungs to breathe…

I look to escape this insane world
to places where art is carved into trees,
and where stores sit in backyards.
A place with music free, uninvited
sounds off beaks of nobled beasts.

I close my eyes and think of waterfalls
to which I bathe and feel the being
close…close to save.

For I reach with wings encaged
and hope he breaks the rings.

To think to fly where material gods don't exist
and to where papers don't merit or sting.

For I reach with wings encaged
and hope he breaks the rings.

So gold his key does dangle,
so white are his wings, I close my eyes,
and towards heavens' skies,
I pray to leave worlds sane.

Beyond the Crossroads lays a Blue Blue Sky

To crossroads we run,
and I question why.
For the trees at these roads block the sun,
and in dizzying circles we do fly.

And in breathlessness
we retreat,
deeper into forest
tripping with tired feet.

And the rains,
the dew from treetops high
casts a pain,
which escapes our eyes that blue blue sky.

And I cry!
Why do we step on our wings,
and not reach, not fly?
For the winds beyond sing.

And the trees there sway
against the mist of ocean's play.

Shackled in a World of Waves

Into depths of soul you searched.
Into these depths blinded in chaos
you plunged, forgetting I was there too.

And I became shackled in this world.
World of waves once white and blue,
drowning with eyes open to the black

Mi Angelo of Light, the Angelo of Flight

This Angelo of light,
this messenger
takes my hand
and guides my spirit to write.

His breath near
warm I feel his touch,
but to my fear
the breath, the touch Vanishes.

I envision this!
For times he is near
I am in bliss,
but his often flight tears.

And to consol my saddened heart
in his fanciful flights,
I picture wings soaring start
to heaven's night bright.

And here he tells
of progress in his steer,
picking up what on me fell.
And tells of a mind growing clear.

Mi Angelo whose flight
casts me the blackest of nights.
The one who takes my hand
and guides my spirit to write.

To consol my saddened heart
in his fanciful flights,
I picture wings soaring start
to heaven's night bright.

Silence Holds What is Secret

Broken is my allegiance but still duty bound,
I walk with you.
The walk's silence holds what is secret.

The silence is broken by children's cries.
But still my heart soars,
with the mock of an Angel.

Float Away

Like a child holding to a helium balloon,
one careless move and the string slips
from your fingers.

Left you are standing to watch
what is so delicate, so beautiful float away.
Float away—Like him.

And I ask, do balloons have a conscience?

He like the Hare

Like a hare still covered in winter coat,
he digs at the earth deep seeking its blue.

And the hare lies within this hole
to escape the drumming heat of the spring sun.

Cut Was Her Hair, Her Freedom

As he cut my baby's hair,
found also cut was my freedom as mother.

My Heart does Cleave

Still naïve,
I stumble
through to which I cleave,
through the forest in which I tumble.

I tumble in what I ignore.
The signs of colored leaves
drifting towards forests' floors,
to which to eyes does please.

And the day grows short
darkening what is behind.
But caught,
still in sweet green grasses I find.

7

I Chose to Dive Through Breaking Waters

Awakened as if in Night

Always awakened I'd drift to sleep,
for the always night is cold and lonely.

My company only stars and moon
but too far away, I could talk but not reach.

And the years would pass
with silent alarms forever ringing.
But the sleep was so inviting.

And on one night equal to revelation,
a night not of time but period of morning wake,
I found another soul wandering.
Wandering with eyes wide open
holding water to the eyes…

And the night sung no longer of cold,
but of warm breezes where feet bare to walk.

And lonely this soul and I became together
helpless to watch those wander in the sleep.

For those who walk in sleep stumble
soaking more of tangible as pills to keep…
Keep the sleep.

And never is enough to keep the forever sleep
so they eat and eat as caterpillars to the leaves.
And the green, the green is losing
by populations gone mad.
For never will there be enough trees.

Heroes Never Sung

An office busy with nonsense
grew silent
with the presence of a little man.

A man only little in stature,
for they truly were the dwarfs.

And the dwarfs' blue eyes pierced
his shy brown.
With his back turned they laughed…
Laughed as children.

They were ignorant to what wasn't same.
And the hero stung at hearts deaf.

He didn't laugh along,
but questioned who they were.
He was only met with silence.
American? Go Home? he asked.

Were they truly American?
For didn't they see, this America of theirs
was of the many as once they.

And shades turned from white to red.
Was it shame or anger?
And this hero was met with silence.

Met with silence…
For what do the sleepers do with real heroes?

The Awakening

It was by the grace of God
I fell into teaching.
For even in college had I not grown.
A self-realization for the evident need
of self-education.

Evident was my ignorance,
a product of society, a lacking in society.

Perhaps born and lost to the Masses
which overpopulation breeds
great minds are lost.

By the grace of God, I found mine.

The Messenger

My guardian,
My gatekeeper,
My median,
who into my skin seeps…

I quested,
sought for truth
boiling under flesh to fester
and ripped away my noose.

My guardian,
My gatekeeper,
My median,
who into my skin seeps…

In Time
granted was my wish,
and like the sands soiled with lime
in truth I was kissed.

My guardian,
My gatekeeper,
My median,
who into my skin seeps…

Awakened,
lost was all that was bliss.
Now in truth I stand too forsaken
and emptied is my dish.

I close my eyes and pray
this is all a dream

in which I lay.
I wake in my own screams.

Who am I?
Where do I belong?
Tightening on me is edges of sky.
Blue lights dancing in blue songs.

Dandelion's Fanning Insistence

Though vast in man's hardware
of asphalt streets,
where black covers once life of green,
weaved in earth tone's seam.

Out peeked a small sun
with body lean.
The ever presence
of wild beauty mean.
Standing high in all resistance!

The dandelion's fanning insistence!

Layered in Beauty

Sweet to the eyes in wishes,
blown to the winds in kisses,
white parachutes take-off uncovers green sun
painting pictures of many births from one.

The dandelion layered in Beauty.

Raft of Comfort

You wade in the raft.
A raft of comfort on softly rocking seas,
drifting to a blissful sleep.
But I chose to dive
through breaking waves…

8

I Pull my Branches until…one is Strong Enough to Lift

From my Tree I Pull its Branches

Washed in the insanity, I reach out to a man
whose world is surrounded by cliffs.

And so cutting his falls, his mind rattles
unable to sift.
And so real the world below becomes.

I lean over his world reaching hands
to pull, to lift…and underneath
quickened becomes the sand.

So easy it would be to walk away
and let him sink in his own drift.
But out of love I stay and watch the horror.

Watch the horror as sands blind him
and his world becomes dark, isolated.
And from my tree I pull its branches
until one is strong enough to lift.

Caught Behind the Bowl

I look and try to seek beyond the glass
which warps my view of his shape, his world.

And in this fishbowl he drowns,
not in the water but what clouds.
Sick, he has become.

But armless he cannot seek to change
the waters.
But outside the fishbowl,
I can fetch for clear water
and throw him to swim.

I Won! Mommy, I Won!

And to a fire engine's whistle
marked their start.
And faster than a pistol
the line was part.

And the Egg hunt began!
to gather the many globes
of color,
and to full to tip.

A bright face of mine
did shine.
And yelled he did,
Mommy, I won!

And pictures snapped
did blare,
for to newspapers he was dared.

In passing flashes
another streak was lit,
for one small girl cried
at her only two blue,
and tipped to hers he did.

And in my heart I declared
as he, I won! Mommy, I won!

Donates of a Child

I watched the red liquid drip drip.
I waited and watched sleeves roll.

I would not be afraid I thought
as I looked towards the cross…red.
My liquid gold I would give.

Those in white scurried and soothed
with talk and sugared drinks and rolls.

And I waited and watched
liquid red, drip, drip.
I held eyes and stomach steady
as sleeves rolled.

My turn and adult in thinking
I was ready to give,
but as a child I was turned away,
for my physique too small
would not sustain the drip, drip
of the red liquid gold.

—*attempting to donate blood*
  but under 110

Sand Dollar

Fragile you sit amongst the rough sands,
amongst the rough sea.

Delicate as life, yet within keeps to Angels.
Five guardians released when shells do break.

And in roughened hands,
hands hold to these wings.

Think of me as one of those angels.
An Angel who holds her hands
to catch your tears.

The Angel to turn tears to rivers' rush,
a rush of strength free of its salts.

So when shells shall break *free* I become
to hold feathered arms, to catch your sad diamonds.

Some Strange Tide

I was amongst His Hope,
a test
of humanity's scope,
His quest.

And by chance
in register's lines,
I caught her aged call's lance,
Miss, Miss would you be so kind?

And a girl turned her way,
and pointed her to pay phones
to catch taxi's play,
to which she found no tone.

And trust I did was instinct,
and helped in my car too low.
I wondered to cities' extinct,
would a return to humanity be a blow?

9

Return I did to Get in Line

Through Another Street I Pass

Through another street I pass
closer still to the end of this journey.

I look towards skies that opened to rains.
The skies that held the black of the night
and held to golden rays.
To the surreal of its purples…reds,
my eyes have found and breathed in.

Walking each street for each year,
which in first years I was pushed,
for I could not walk.
Then in youth I ran and had at times been lost.

To paces slow, to paces fed,
I wonder to where, to who
my knees will be for bled?

Odin

In modest shame, I lay you upon my breast,
dear Odin.
For not so tame has been my quest
and kneel I have for Bragi.

He sends me all I should ornately write,
dear Odin.
But for your swords I fall
and cut I am into your night.

Idunn I am and hold those golden apples
as I do mine.
And do I seek those new to sample
and taste you do of that sweet wine.

Oh, Odin you call me in my dreams
and kiss my brow, and shed your wings.
I call for you to take me now!

Oh Odin, you offer more,
and in windows secret
quietly they keep score.
For my heart thrashes for what's kept.

To Bragi,
evermore...
my knees are soaked now of blood
from this journey lore
with your floods.

And did he, my Odin hold to me
so that I had not sunk but set those floods free.

Shall my Odin carry me,
I would shed my anchor
and close my ears to your maddened pleas.

or is it all the same?

Gods taken from Norse Mythology
Most prominent with the Vikings 8th & 9th centuries

Odin—is the All-God, god of poetry, culture, art, war, Wisdom; God not
*   to men but warriors & kings*

Bragi—the son of Odin is the god of poetry & eloquence

Indunn—consort or wife of Bragi, she was the goddess of eternal youth,
*   carrying the basket of apples for aging gods & goddesses-*

Star

He asked foolishly what it felt like
to be a star.
Just a Star of the day,
but still to him a star.

Did he think my ego
would sing?

I answered, I felt like a boat
on unchartered waters.
For the reward was great,
yet greatly saddening.

For as a boat new, I knew not
if my seams would keep.
Or if the salts would sting
testing seams strength?

Unchartered, I may just indeed sink.

For as a boat starred,
lighted am I
to be seen from afar.

Seen afar in frailties, which do scorn.

The Cat Dish

If your eyes are open you can find answers
in life's everyday routine.
I was questioning my path…

My three-year old daughter
was feeding our two cats
one orange and one black.
Both had a designated dish.

This one morning there was confusion
and from what was simple became profound.
"Henry, you're eating out of the wrong dish!"

And my wish…
I saw was to eat, to nourish
with the right dish.

That morning…
clear I do remember,
it was the noise, the loudness of children
that threw off the cat's knowing.

And as quiet returned so did instinct
And fed was his hunger, as one could predict.

The Quest

He sang as Don Quixote
disillusioned and insane
in poetry and in quest.

Posed was the sanity of poets.
There is none
and I sat in happy blame.

For my quest
is not to the many,
but sits in my dreams that came.

To the many who wonder of poets' quests
and shake their heads in utter disgust.
They think the dreams only pain,
but in worlds of play in this I stay sane.

For to touch is not enough, I seek to feel
what is said not exists.
And in this, I walk and persist.

And he sang as Don Quixote
and in my seat of theatre,
I became the stage,
for he sang to what to me does page.

And you ask what that may be?
To what songs do poets dance?

It is to see what stands not as reality
but what flitters on perchance.

The perchance I just may be Don Quixote.

—April 18, 2003
  The Man of La Mancha, NY

Under the Lights I do Belong

I sat in my seat comfortable
in heavy jacket to quietly take it all in.

But I heard my name called,
and the voice loomed calling me to stage.

And that jacket I shed…

And I walked weak
hearing the click, click
of my shoes in the quiet
until I reached the stage.

The lights blared
and I could not see my audience,
so I sought to find my voice and did.

And I did roar under the blinding light
bringing my song to the void.
It was a void only because I could not see,
for indeed there were spectators.

I returned to that seat hearing the distance
of the click, click of my shoes…

And this seat now cold
was no longer of comfort,
for it's on the stage, under the lights
I do belong!

—February 22, 2003
Nubian Poet Society, "Open Mic"
Manasquan, NJ

With Him to My Back

Twas the dream of freedom
and of winds through my hair
on Harley's I did dare.

And with him to my back,
not to his, I did fly!

And through mountains of dark greens,
through the dark of night we ran.

Without helmets both heads of hair did fly!

A Heaven in Jamaica

Passing papers airborne
write I would who we are.
And caught in lines to justify, justify
to Custom's Gatekeeper I indeed exist,
found I was blind.

Blanks stood and I was sent away.
I would find the time to self-identify.
Simply after, return I did, to get in line.

With a smile gleaming so white
she was satisfied.
And crossed I did to a land once forbid,
a land with skies and seas blue.

A land with fruited trees, a land named
as the land of food and water.

—*Jamaica's Airport—5/18/03*
  The Gatekeeper black & she

The Perfect Shell

Combing beaches for shells,
I searched for the priceless, the exotic,
shells that had washed ashore unscathed.

Combing beaches I hoped not to pass
one by.
The search became painful
for each inch was sore to the eye.
Then upon hope I saw the one shell I so sought.

A shell stood as one with the most surface.
The shell sang to me…
perhaps not every shell was for me to find.

—Jamaica, May 2003

The Most Beautiful Shell

Some shells stand perfect in that they are whole.
Some beautiful even though broke,
for once they had been so exuberant,
so fantastic.

I choose the beautiful and broke,
for I find it is more exotic and beautiful
than those that stood perfect and plain.

The beauty escapes what lays intact,
for it was left untouched.

—*Jamaica, May 2003*

The Scars of Ballerina Toes

Most times the scars remain unseen
but when the sun touches my skin,
when it goes from white to brown,
faint fans of circles white cross my toes as bridge.

It is a reminder of the dance
when I learned the magic of toe.
Naïve I believed ballerinas could fly…
fly on magic toes.
But stood they did with help of wooden shoes
where virgin toes bleed into cotton.

The circles stood as a reminder of the dance.
A reminder of what I gave up.

I Believe

God gives us the opportunities
but in the end,
I believe the ultimate god
is ourselves…

10

She Grew as a Dandelion
Wile and Unfixed

Armed with Seed

Armed with pesticides
all those cultivated
stack against the dandelions.

But the dandelions
do not play their game,
for they take stance
and bomb only with seeds.

The Field of Hearts

And Rumi spoke of a place that was
"Out beyond ideas of wrongdoing and right doing."
Speaking of this field, which we should meet.

To the ears it sounded of Utopia,
but it wasn't enough,
for my field grew hearts only touched
by enough sun…
Only touched by enough rains
to sustain their beauty.

And my place was out beyond false pride,
where fields of hearts grew in forgiveness.

In my place only could the ground feed,
knowing the knowledge of the field
where limbo doesn't sustain
but has felt wrongdoing and right doing.

And past the gates of pride I walked
and closed behind.
It is in this field I wait and watch for latches to break.
Take this road and I'll meet you there.

In this field, hearts are never lost
to the disease called pride.

—*4/29/03*
   Rumi—13th century Persian mystic poet
   Famed poet in Hindu mysticism

In Seas of Forgiveness

In dreams by the palm trees we met.
I reached to grasp a piece of sea glass,
and I placed it in his hands.
The sea glass to stand as a symbol,
that I had been washed
in the seas of forgiveness,
and no longer do I cut sharp.

By the Hands of Mini-gods

Behind moving clouds of gray,
the oranges did play
off the fullness of its face.

And danced it did in colors
hanging above what seemed
only as feet.

Above the city's skyline
all those manmade lights
as spectacular as they are,
still were outshined.

Outshined by what stands real,
for its face lit from Gods of Suns.
Cast my eyes were and drawn
back to the florescent lights beneath,
made by hands of mini-gods.

—April 18, 2003
Driving Back from the Theatre
taking in NYC's skyline
sitting under a full moon

I Walk Upon Jewels

Through my hands the sand to be tumbles.
The ocean's hardened jewels.
The colors dazzle in browns, soft, red, bright,
and the whites greened or clear.

The black shines brighter than night,
like coal.
Through my hands this sand tumbles
sifting through beach worn hands.

I turn these jewels to my gemstones
that are more than to wear,
for I walk upon them with my feet,
and anchor in my worth.

Roots grow Seed

Roots I found grow seed.
If planted with Ivy,
it is all the harder to seek light.

For roots I found grow seed.
And clipped I had at mine
and spring forth life I did.

But awakened…
I seek new soils to plant,
for old soil sat unturned.
The fires that lay beneath do churn,
and shovel they did to burn.

And in three-way mirrors I blinked,
for roots I found grow seed.

So Weary my Heart

My legs so weary from this walk
I turn to water and bathe I do this pain.

So weary my soul,
to sleep, I escape and lay to pillows.
So weary my heart,
I embrace my children to fill.

I rest so I may not avert
but continue my journey.

Waves of Gold

I squint over a wheel held straight
at the waves before me,
in the heat dancing off yellow lines
painted to black roads.

And drive I do over the black
to reach at rainbows' waves of gold.

Profoundly Mild

Kept is the hair long and wild,
for when the winds blow with dance
brushing skins profoundly mild,
I remember in my sleep,
I am alive!

Wild She Wears Whites and Yellows

She grew as a dandelion, wild and unfixed.
A Flower seen amongst those cultivated as weed.

But still she stood stronger than those as beautiful.
For through her veins flowed the simple rains
and unaltered sun.

When her yellow face grew white
not death was carried but seed.
The seed would fly leaving her roots
never stationary, with birth to numbers.

The numbers of wild white to the winds…

—*May 7, 2003*

Fallen Trees

Along the shore of its sandy beaches,
palms and fruited trees upturned
and lay with roots exposed.

But still, branches held green,
for enough water still fed its roots.

—*Jamaica, May 2003*

11

I Call to God! Send us your Saints

American Pearl

The headlines read
"We are prepared!"
My eyes are led
to an age filled of terror fed.

Biochemical…
and thoughts return to ancient plagues.
Empirical,
carried is a soul on invisible legs.

"We are prepared!"
And vaccines
will be bled
to go about life silently taxing.

And tonight,
we will see autocracy unfurl
as the President holds switches to light,
holding to a notion of American pearl.

Dear God…
Our soldiers on standby for whim,
save humanity,
for the good stands slim,
and release us from this scrutiny!

—*March 17, 2003*
  St. Patrick's day
  I call to God!
  "Send us your Saints!"

"A" for Human's Arrogance

The words fell off lips of my baby.
One I brought in with a mother's hope.

"What is war?"
And to find answers at my heart tore,
for I myself question
these letters…W…A…R…
that only forms a word,
for terms are still unclear.

I think W stands for its wake,
A for humans' arrogance,
and R for humans' regrets.

But these words even to me stand large.
"Son…I believe it is when we
fight to keep out the bad."

"Mommy, do people die?"
"Yes, sometimes they do."

"Then Mommy,
how are we keeping out the bad?"
I shake my head for I haven't really got a clue.

And I Stand Tall knowing...

Near the cities,
near the power plants,
in despair, in pity,
I hope the world recants.

Is WWIII on horizons?
Will my children grow to marry?
I remember WWII's Germans and Pisans.
Who with us will carry?

My lover...
My life!
Can I pray he runs for cover?
Pray that bullets miss, so I may someday be his wife.

Near the ports
and the bases
only miles we sit apart.
I hold faith looking on...to my children's faces.

And we wait
but not all.
In ignorance they walk unquestioning fate,
and I stand tall.
Stand tall knowing
with tears flowing,
and pray if we fall
that we be graced with the haste of War's call.

—*March 18, 2003*

Wealth Set Afire in Face-off

Wealth set afire in face-off.
Lined are their skies black with smoke.

The pools of ugly black
which bent many men's hands green,
which suffocated life in the very waters
that give life.

I can't say I'd be sad to see them destroyed,
for the ugly black pools accost us severely.
Reaching they do with ungodly hands all too slick.
In this ugly black pool men do slip.

—In the midst of war in Iraq
  The people burning oil fields
  2003'

What Underneath Cowers

I wake and the first day of Spring is beautiful.
Cut are any brisk winds within my castle walls.
Fences break, making for a warm backyard.

But in the background through TV,
I hear other worlds shake.
And I take in the same crisp blue sky
that masked the many lives
taken down in two towers.

In their backyard today,
do their skies mask what underneath cowers?

—*March 22, 2003*

The Knife of False Pride

Holding to the knife of false pride,
he cuts not one throat but two.

12
He Answers to Any Name

A Dandelion Amongst the Grass

Bright amongst the green or soft
like a whisper of a ghost,
I call in quiet out to you to wander.

To wander the field and pick me,
to blow with quivering lips,
my seeds to the wind.

Blue Lights of Love

I thought the blues only existed for lovers,
but laying side by side,
between mother and daughter,
those blue lights swept.

Following Paths Strewn

In family tradition
followed they did,
the colored strings' addiction,
in delight to adults' forbid.

And fell it did from balls of yarn
that ran long and curved,
and rolled in not was torn.
Little fingers rolled in what at times did swerve.

For what was strewn
lay behind, over, and beyond.

And to destinations' end
sat globes of color in tune
to blend...
the symbols of spring's new blooms.

Those globes primary
to what wheels.
The globes gathered to baskets by visionaries
with faces glowing and squeals.

For what is strewn
lays behind, over, and beyond.

—*Easter, 2003'*
   Easter egg game—children
   wake to a ball of yarn strewn which
   inevitably leads them to their
   basket of eggs

Globes

Just what hangs from this tree of life?
The globes of knowledge?
Of our awakening?

I reach for the green ball
that dangles out of reach,
as upon my birth was my death of consciousness.

I climb for the midnight blue
that remembers and sparkles in this truth.

I then reach for the yellow
as soft as the mellow glow
of the luminescent moon,
and to my fingertips I feel its pull.

And low sits the red still glowing in its ashes,
but too hot to touch I move my ladder.

I reach for the white that holds the water.
This globe is ethereal and in it,
I soak in its nourishment.

And as it disappears,
a black globe disillusions the eye
hanging not as negative but for the night.

And I grasp this last globe
and take this with me to sleep,
to dream of treetops where heavens meet.

Hands of Blue Lights

Closed are my eyes
and blue lights dance,
as long drawn out sighs
caught out of my chance.

They surge with form encircling
as a smoker might draw rings,
as crowns might fling
to unseen Kings.

But the blue changes form
and into Hands
pressed to stop they storm,
saddened to failed plans.

In Day to Walk, In Night to Soar

To my eyes I define,
for you are never half.
Never as boat's adrift line,
you stand with staff.

I seek to grasp for hands
fleshed under broken wings.
To walk with, through, strange lands,
to where our beauty brings.

In day to walk,
in night to soar,
against babbling talk
with light as core.

Seek my Side,
for never here you are half.
He calls us back still as Bride
with rings of blue circles, surrounding staffs.

I hear His calls
of beauty, of want,
in the snowflakes that fall,
in the ocean's roaring front.

In day to walk,
in night to soar,
against the babbling talk
with my children as core.

Perception is what perception holds.
Tangible,
you stand as whole…
fallen Angel.

Look Side to Side

Look side to side,
for following straight paths do blind.
Yet hear my voice cast.

Guiding you still to walk straight,
more is gained with many eyes,
building as many states,
for in which one lie.

Look side to side,
but seek my voice.
It can't be denied
as choice.

That who Enchants my Sleep

My skin chills as I think of these dreams,
these visits.

From where did he come?
From where did he run?
Is it this earthly air he breathes?

Unseen at times, my flesh speaks of his presence
as these airs follow my spine.
I close my eyes and pray
seeing the wondrous purple violets which enflame.

My head swims with this and know I do of more,
for I was sent an angel who enchants my sleep
night and in the light of day.

And when he speaks, he speaks as if he was fallen,
but I see what is bright and reach I do to touch.
Touching to disarm what seems surreal.

He enchants my sleep day and night,
and reach I do and feel…

Three Hands that stand as Doors

Still soul searching, I asked God to guide me
and He has.

How can I ignore blatant signs from Him?
I stand trying to decipher what it means.

It was not done by my hand
but perhaps one or more of three,
and I dust for prints.

Handed Breath

At the alter
her hands spoke
as words without falter.
A testimony to faith spoke.

And lean in her black dress
stood contrast,
to offer contest
brought louder to her white robe.

For in silence
one can still hear,
for no penance
to any is clear.

To even the deaf
stands no test,
for in the signer's handed breath
souls of the listeners may rest.

—May 25, 2003
  Baptism—with a sign language interpreter present
  Testimony and sign to my faith
  that even physical loss of hearing can't
  prevent those from hearing

My Mutable God

I love my mutable God
for He answers to any name
his people choose to call.

Fields of Dandelions

And through fields of
dandelions towards infinity,
I find.

I Believe in Fairy Tales

There is enough that lies within me
to weight the world's dreams.

I believe in Fairy Tales…

More Books?

My little one asked why write another book.
I answered,
"It is my play."

About the Author

Christine Redman-Waldeyer is the author of
I Swim Seas of Thirty-Two Legions, poetry book, iUniverse,
November 2002, *The Talisman Pick "Voices and Hats,"*
poetry book, iUniverse, December 2002, *The Land of the Frogs—
"Seas of Green,"* iUniverse February 2003, and
Around the World with Rosalie, a pre-K children's book,
Dorrance Publishing, July 2003.

She is a life-long resident of Manasquan, New Jersey
currently teaching as a professor and instructor
of history and business, Ocean County College
and Stuart School of Business Administration.

She holds her degree in English, Georgian Court College,
her Masters in Liberal Arts, Monmouth University
and is currently working on her Doctorate
of Arts & Letters, Drew University. Much of her
work is based on her experiences as a clairvoyant reader
working with the supernatural and investigation into dreams. This
interest has also led her to explore and study histories
of religion and the spiritual world.

For comments or questions
contact the author at crpetey@hotmail.com

978-0-595-28267-8
0-595-28267-9